REFLECTIONS ON A RIVER

A COLOUR PORTFOLIO OF THE MERSEY'S SHIPPING

Paul Boot & Nigel Bowker

Copyright © P. Boot, N. Bowker & Priam Publications 1993

Revised and Reprinted in the United Kingdom in 1995
by John & Marion Clarkson,
18 Franklands, Longton, Preston PR4 5PD
ISBN 0 9521179 3 2

Originally published in the United Kingdom in 1993 by
Priam Publications
as ISBN 0 9521133 0 9

Printed by Amadeus Press Ltd., Huddersfield, Yorkshire

FRONT COVER

A wonderfully evocative summer morning's view of the river in the late 1950's as the Canadian Pacific liner Empress of Britain *leaves the Prince's Landing Stage assisted by four Alexandra tugs, with a fascinating selection of steam tugs arrayed in the foreground. From left to right these are the* **East Cock** *(1909),* **Nelson** *(1935),* **Bramley Moore** *(1922) and the* **North End** *(1957). There are almost as many tugs visible in this view as the total number in service on the river today. Just visible on the extreme right alongside the landing stage is the Isle of Man steamer* Ben-My-Chree *of 1927.* J.M. Williams

REAR COVER   *14.12.74*

High water and winter sunshine looking South from Alfred Pier Head. A strong North Westerly – has created lively conditions in the estuary, so the situation at the exposed Mersey Bar will be far worse, with the result that the Bar pilot boat has abandoned the station to seek shelter in the Sloyne. A ferry is departing Woodside for Liverpool, whilst one of the two 70ft pilot launches lies at the north end of the ferry stage. N.P.B.

CLAN MACLAREN   1946   6,389grt   The Clan Line Steamers Ltd.   *2.5.74*

The Indian Summer of the Traditional Cargo Liner

The evening sunlight reflecting off the rivetted hull plates of the **Clan Maclaren** *betrays the age of this elderly cargo-liner. By then 28 years old, she would normally have been replaced by more modern tonnage but, like many of her counterparts under the British flag, she had been retained in the run up to containerisation of their services. She was finally withdrawn in 1976 and sold for further service. The 1953 built* **Laomedon** *of Blue Funnel Lines, laying on the far side of the dock, was sold, also for further trading, the following year.* P.H.B.

INTRODUCTION

The post-war era has seen many changes and, cynics might argue, few for the better. Certainly this is true of the shipping industry which, particularly in the last thirty years has been through a dramatic, and to those involved, traumatic period of evolution. The British merchant fleet, once the largest in the world has now diminished to the extent that to say it had been decimated would, for once, be an understatement. Not only have the ships gone but so too have the shipowners. Who, at the beginning of the 1960's could have foreseen that such once eminent concerns as Blue Funnel, Brocklebank, Clan, Henderson and Port Lines, to recall but a few, would now be just memories, with the shipping interests of other long standing companies considerably reduced or disposed of entirely? Radical advances in the conveyance and handling of cargoes, the emergence of the subsidised fleets of newly independent nations and the increasing tendency of operators to place their vessels under various flags of convenience, thereby taking advantage of reduced manning and operating costs, are just some of the many factors that have each, in their way, contributed to this decline.

The ships themselves have also undergone a radical transformation, with much of the conventional tonnage replaced by specialist carriers that have little of the elegance or form of their forebears. Containerships and bulk carriers have now largely usurped the cargo-liners and humble tramp steamers that once brought in a diverse range of cargoes and carried Britain's exports to destinations throughout the world. The pattern of coastal shipping has experienced similar changes, with the proliferation of ro-ro ferries reflecting the country's every growing dependence on road transport. Perhaps the saddest loss has been the graceful ocean liners which were never to regain the glories of the 'twenties and 'thirties and received a death blow with the advent of the jet airliner.

Not surprisingly it was throughout the traditional ports, steeped in history and long established labour intensive practices, that these changes were to be felt with the greatest vengeance and no more so than at Liverpool and Manchester, where the transition has at times been a painful affair. The fortunes of the Mersey's ports have in many ways largely mirrored those of the industries of the north-west region. Closure of major manufacturing establishments, including Tate & Lyle's sugar refinery, the steelworks at Shotton and Irlam and more generally the Lancashire textile mills have, in each instance, resulted in the loss of significant tonnages of imported raw materials and, to a lesser extent, exported finished products. Further losses have come over these years with the focus of trade gradually shifting to the east coast as integration into the European Community has displaced our former Colonial and Commonwealth ties.

The port has survived, however, albeit entrenched mainly at the northern end of the Liverpool system, where the construction of the Seaforth Dock in the early 'seventies with its container, grain and timber terminals, has enabled the larger carriers to be handled. As for the remainder, the South Docks have long since closed to commercial traffic and few craft are ever to be seen south of Huskisson Dock in the northern section. Birkenhead Docks are now a mere shadow of their former selves and on the Manchester Ship Canal only a handful of berths remain in use, with little activity beyond Runcorn. The Mersey Docks and Harbour Company continues however to fight the tide of recession and is actively developing the Freeport project, most recently in the Birkenhead system. With the opening of the Channel Tunnel it is predicted that there will be a resurgence of trade, with the Mersey's preferential location as an Atlantic bridgehead again exploited to the full. Regrettably the past cannot be recreated and whatever the future brings, we will never again see the wonderful variety of shipping that once filled the docks and graced the river.

We have attempted, however, in this book to recall something of those days and have brought together as representative a selection of photographs as availability of suitable material has allowed. From the outset, one of the principal considerations was that all photographs that were to be included must have been taken within the confines of the river and the docks. Resisting the temptation on several occasions to step beyond these boundaries, this aim has been achieved. Inevitably there are omissions and it has not proved possible to include some of the famous names that have been associated with the Mersey. It must be remembered though that only thirty years ago, colour photography had yet to achieve the standards, and popularity, it has today. Its few exponents had to contend with a limited range of slow speed films, not many of which have stood the test of time. We are deeply indebted, therefore, to those photographers who have so kindly allowed a number of historic views from their collections to be included here and have also provided help and assistance in many other ways. To H.B. Christiansen, John Clarkson, Malcolm McRonald, Alan Spedding, Bill Vasey and John Williams, a sincere thank you. For those interested in the equipment and materials used, the majority of the photographs were taken on Pentax cameras, mainly on Kodachrome films (principally Kodachrome II and its successor Kodachrome 25) with the remainder generally on Agfa CT 18.

Paul H. Boot
Nigel P. Bowker
Wirral – March 1993

PORT PIRIE   1947   10,535 grt.   Port Line Ltd.

15.11.71

Something of the atmosphere of the north Liverpool docks as they were is captured in this study of the twin screw motorship **Port Pirie** *being manoeuvred onto her berth in Huskisson Branch Dock No. 3 by Alexandra Towing Company's tugs, with the* **North Rock** *prominent alongside. She had just arrived from Whangarei, New Zealand, with a cargo of refrigerated and other produce. In the background are representatives of several of the companies associated with the port. Harrison Line's* **Magician** *can be seen immediately behind the* **Port Pirie***, on the west side of Huskisson Dock. Beyond, in the adjoining Canada Dock, are the* **Majestic** *of Shaw Savill & Albion Co. Ltd. and the Blue Funnel liner* **Patroclus***. Further up in the system the* **Bennachie** *of the Ben Line Steamers Ltd., can be seen in Brocklebank Dock and in the far distance the* **Rockhampton Star** *of the Blue Star Line Ltd., can just be discerned.*

P.H.B.

3

AUREOL   1951   14,083 grt.   Elder Dempster Lines Ltd.   **and**

One of the last of the Liverpool liners languishes between voyages in Brocklebank Branch Dock in the company of the Booker Viking. *The Aureol's two older and smaller consorts on the West African run, the* Accra *and* Apapa, *had both been withdrawn towards the end of the 1960's leaving her to maintain the service single handed. Early in 1972 her sailings were transferred to Southampton but by 1974 the service had become uneconomic and her sale to Panamanian interests came at the end of that year. Renamed* Marianna VI *she was used as an accommodation ship initially at Jeddah and later at Rabegh some miles to the north on the Saudi Red Sea coast.*

BOOKER VIKING   1967   5,383 grt.   Booker Line Ltd.   6.11.71

The Booker Line had a long established service between Georgetown and Liverpool, principally concerned with the importation of sugar from the Guayanan estates. The Booker Viking *was one of a number of new vessels introduced during the 1960's when the transition was made from bagged to bulk shipments and the service extended to Antigua, St. Kitts and Surinam. In 1980 she was sold to the Qatar National Navigation & Transport Co. Ltd. and renamed* Al Amirah. *As such she arrived at Gadani Beach, Pakistan, in February 1986 for demolition.*

4

P.H.B.

QUEEN ELIZABETH 2   1969   66,450 grt.   Cunard Line Ltd.

24.7.90

Cunard's transatlantic passenger sailings from Liverpool ended in 1967, with the conventional cargo service following not long after. Their colours were to be seen in force again on the river when the Queen Elizabeth 2, making a special cruise around Britain to celebrate Cunard's 150th anniversary, called to commemorate the inaugural sailing from the port by the Britannia in July 1840. Her visit coincided with a perfect warm sunny day, drawing large crowds to view her at anchor off the Pier Head and providing the ferries with an excellent day's takings.
Following her exploits as a troopship during the Falklands conflict and the continuing

problems with the steam turbine machinery, the Q.E. 2 was re-engined at Bremerhaven during the winter of 1986/7. Nine 6 cylinder diesel engines were installed, each coupled to a generator set driving electric propulsion motors connected to each of the twin-screw shafts; an arrangement that has enabled the original service speed of 28.5 knots to be maintained with considerable savings in fuel costs. At the same time a new, broader funnel was fitted. Thus rejuvenated it is to be hoped that the future of the last of the great North Atlantic Liners will be secured for some years to come.

P.H.B.

A Bygone Era – Pier Head scene. 1961

Much has changed since this view was taken. Canadian Pacific's **Empress of Britain** *(1956/25,516 grt) is approaching Prince's Landing Stage to take on passengers, having moved up from the company's cargo berth at Gladstone Dock. Already berthed on the stage are the Liverpool & North Wales S.S. Co. Ltd's* **St. Tudno** *preparing for a 10.45 departure to Llandudno, in her penultimate year of service before her owners went into liquidation; and Lamey's first motor tug* **John Lamey** *whose funnel is just visible to the left of the gable end of Riverside Railway station. The* **Empress** *is attended by the steam tug* **Canning** *at the stern and the new motor tug is in all probability the* **Gower** *– on trials before taking up station at Port Talbot, whilst one of Rea's early 50's Aberdeen built steamers is just ahead of the* **St. Tudno***. In South West Prince's Dock, the Belfast S.S. Co.*

Ltd.'s freighter **Ulster Premier** *(1955/979 grt) is working cargo using her own gear. This narrow southward extension of Prince's Dock was originally part of the passage through to George's Dock on whose site Liverpool's famous trio of waterfront landmarks now stand. Upon closure of George's Dock, the passage became a graving dock, subsequently reverting to a normal wet dock in 1938, and then being infilled during 1965 to provide extra hardstanding in readiness for the introduction of the Belfast car ferry service . Note the period advertisement hoardings featuring paintings of the Belfast and Dublin night mailboats which berthed in West and East Prince's Dock respectively and the British Railways Scammel Scarab 'mechanical horse' laden with crates proceeding down St. Nicholas Place.*

N.P.B. collection

A SELECTION OF LIVERPOOL'S LINERS:

Top:– *Alongside the Prince's Landing Stage is the Cunard passenger cargo liner* Media *(1947/13,345 grt) the first Atlantic passenger vessel to be equipped with stabilisers. She was sold in 1961 to the Italian Codegar Line and, after a major rebuild, emerged as the cruise ship* Flavia. *Later renamed* Flavian, *then* Lavia, *she was gutted by fire at Hong Kong in 1989 and subsequently broken up. Astern is the* Cilicia *(1938/11,172 g) of Anchor Line, one of three similar vessels employed on their service to India and Pakistan and, after withdrawal in 1966, she survived in a static role for training stevedores at Rotterdam until 1980 under the name* Jan Backx.

Bottom:– *The* Prome *(1937/7,043 grt) and her sistership* Salween *each had provision for 75 first-class passengers on Henderson Line's service to Burma. Both were steamships built by Denny Bros. and were withdrawn and sold for demolition in 1962.*

Top:– *The* Britannic *(1930/27,666 grt) was one of the last liners to be built for the White Star Line, which had been merged with Cunard in 1934, and she was to be the last survivor from their fleet when withdrawn in 1960. This graceful two funnel vessel, which retained her White Star colours to the end, epitomised the Harland & Wolff motorships of that era and, together with her near sistership the* Georgic, *were when built, the largest and most powerful of these.*

Bottom:– *The quadruple screw* Reina Del Pacifico *(1931/17,707 grt) was another Harland & Wolff built motorship and she was to serve her owners, the Pacific S.N. Co. Ltd., until 1958. Apart from deployment during the war, principally as a troopship, her entire career was spent on their service between Liverpool and the West Coast of South America.*

7

SOUTHERN CROSS   1955   19,313 grt   Shaw Savill & Albion Co. Ltd.

7.8.71

The Southern Cross made a number of cruises from Liverpool in 1971. The departure of the last of these was on a Saturday afternoon and provided an excellent opportunity to capture her as she swung down river after leaving the berth on the Prince's Landing Stage. Built in 1955 for Shaw Savill's round the world passenger only service, she was innovative in several respects, not least in having the engines positioned aft. Designed as a one-class ship, the **Southern Cross** was joined by a near sister, the **Northern Star**, in 1962 which sailed in the opposite, eastwards, direction. By the end of that decade, however, the service was becoming increasingly unviable and the Southern Cross spent her last years under the British flag cruising, finally being withdrawn in 1972. Sold the following year, renamed Calypso and extensively refitted, this was to herald a new career. Now sailing under her fifth name as the Liberian flagged **Ocean Breeze** and well into her fortieth year of service, she remains largely unaltered externally. Her consort, the **Northern Star**, was not to be so fortunate, however, having been consigned to the breakers in 1975.

P.H.B.

8

KINNAIRD CASTLE, CUSTODIAN & IDOMENEUS

30.6.73

The Alfred Lock entrance to the Birkenhead system restricts movements of larger vessels to the period within two hours up to high water and to overcome these limitations the adjoining Alfred Dock can be used in the manner of a half-tide basin. With this dock levelled with the river, ships departing or arriving may do so without the need to lock through individually and thus a greater amount of traffic can be dealt with in the limited time available. It was not uncommon on a good tide to have five, or very occasionally more, sailings or dockings, and sometimes even both. On this Saturday afternoon representatives of three of the principal Lines using Birkenhead are secured in Alfred

Basin as this is brought back up to the level of the rest of the system. Nearest the camera is Union Castle's **Kinnaird Castle** *(1956/7,737 grt) formerly the* **Clan Ross** *of the associated Clan Line Steamers on whose service she would have been running. Behind are the* **Custodian** *(1961/8,847 grt) one of the Harrison Line ships equipped with a Stülcken heavy-lift derrick, and the* Idomeneus *(1949/7,431 grt) of Blue Funnel Line. The swing bridge, just partially visible in the foreground, has now been removed and of the Four Bridges, only one now remains in operation.*

DEFENDER   1955   8,367 grt.   T. & J. Harrison Ltd.

5.9.70

The Birkenhead Docks, unlike the Liverpool system which developed along the river front, were built following the meandering course of the Wallasey Pool, a natural tidal inlet extending two miles inland. In this 1970 aerial view from the West Float, the Defender is near to completing loading for East African ports on the joint Harrison – Hall Line berth. In the distance a number of ships can be seen in the East Float with its extensive grain storage silos and flour mills, Vittoria Dock, and beyond, in Alfred Dock.   The Anglican Cathedral, still under construction is prominent on the Liverpool skyline and the Liver Buildings, St. John's beacon and the Roman Catholic Metropolitan Cathedral can be easily

identified. Much has changed in the intervening years, not least the demolition of the Rank's Ocean Flour Mills from which the photograph was taken. No doubt further changes can be expected as the Birkenhead freeport project develops.
As for the Defender, she was sold by Harrison's in 1975 becoming the Euromariner under the Greek flag. Two years later a major engine failure brought about her demise at Barranquila, Colombia, South America, where she was subsequently demolished.

P.H.B.

CHEVIOT 1961 13,082 grt. Bamburgh Shg. Co. Ltd (W.A. Souter & Co. Ltd.)

18.10.70

The Cheviot was one of four ore carriers owned by Bamburgh Shipping Co. Ltd., a concern established in a partnership between the Newcastle Shipowners, W.A. Souter & Co. Ltd., and the British Iron & Steel Corporation, to whom the vessels were placed on long term charter. The splendid funnel markings, incorporating a castle emblem, offset the invariably rust streaked hulls. On termination of the charter, the Cheviot was sold to Greek owners and as the Dapo Trader occasionally returned to Birkenhead.

Dominating the scene are the three massive gantry unloaders on the north side of Bidston Dock. These were erected in 1952 when the terminal was constructed to handle the

imported ore shipments to the new iron making facility at the Shotton Steelworks of John Summers on Deeside. With over 1.5 million tonnes of ore passing through the berth annually, there were few occasions when there was not at least one vessel discharging there. Following the closure of the steelmaking section of the Shotton Works in 1980 the terminal was occasionally used for discharging bulk cargoes, most notably imported coal for the power stations, but latterly the cranes had stood idle for several years and late in 1992 they were dismantled for scrap.

CLAN MACLAY 1949 6,388 grt. The Clan Line Steamers Ltd.

31.12.74

Under a leaden sky, a wintry sun fleetingly casts a coppery glow over the river as the Clan Maclay *leaves Birkenhead at the beginning of another voyage to East Africa. It is unlikely that this New Year's Eve scene would have been appreciated by those on board the Glasgow registered ship and the celebrations that night would necessarily have been a restrained affair.*

The Clan Maclay, *like most of the Clan Line vessels, was delivered by the Greenock Dockyard Co. Ltd., a subsidiary of the company. The last of a series of six vessels spearheading the post-war reconstruction of the fleet, the* Clan Maclay *was one of the*

four to be powered by a 6 cylinder oilengine, steam turbines being chosen for the remaining pair. The three sets of heavy, paired and cross-tied samson posts gave them a substantial appearance and the excellence of construction was borne out by their long service with the company, the motorships lasting up to 30 years each. All were to be sold in 1976 in what had by then become the terminal run-down of the parent British & Commonwealth Group's shipping interests. The Clan Maclay *traded for a further three years under the Panamanian flag as the* Climax Amethyst *and was broken up at Kaohsiung in June 1979 as the* Angelos.

P.H.B.

AULICA 1960 12,321 grt. Shell Tankers Ltd.

13.7.74.

There can be few places to rival the old Eastham ferry, or the waterfront of the country park, for photographing or just watching shipping, as this glimpse through the trees of the Shell Tanker Aulica, *being escorted up to the lock entrance by the Rea tug* Beechgarth, *illustrates.*

Shell operated an extensive fleet of intermediate size tankers at this time comprised largely of the "H/K" class steam turbine powered ships built in profusion during the 1950's and the later, more stylish development of these, the "A" class. With their dimensions approaching the maximum that could be accommodated on the Manchester Ship

Canal, they were used extensively to serve the Stanlow Refinery bringing in feedstocks and for distributing refined products. The Aulica *was typical of the majority of the "A" class in having turbine propulsion and a separate bridge structure located amidships, although several were built as motorships, and two with composite structures situated aft. With much of their work increasingly being handled by super tankers and specialised product carriers, most of the "H/K" class were disposed of during the 1970's with the "A"s following on through the next decade. In December 1984, a few days before Christmas, the* Aulica *was delivered to Pakistani breakers at Gadani Beach.*

P.H.B.

CITY OF LEEDS   1950   7,622 grt.   Ellerman Lines Ltd

Riding high in the water on her return down the Manchester Ship Canal, the City of Leeds presents an unusual appearance with her truncated funnel as she passes by Moore Village between Warrington and Runcorn. As with many of the larger vessels, the top masts and upper funnel section had been removed in order to meet the height restriction imposed by the bridges over the canal. A special crane berth was provided at Eastham where this operation was carried out, and many of the regular traders to the canal had telescopic or folding mast sections to reduce the time spent here to a minimum. Although not visible in this view, the funnel top has been stowed on the afterdeck, but in many instances

these were stored on the quay at the crane berth where they provided an interesting, if at times difficult, exercise in ship identification. Built as the City of Ottawa for Hall Line, a constituent of Ellerman Lines, she had become the City of Leeds earlier in 1971 in an interchange of names in order to provide appropriate titles for the three vessels placed on the newly introduced Canadian City Line service. She was one of the last steamers to remain in the fleet when sold in 1975 to the Gulf Shipping Group. Retaining the British flag as the Gulf Venture, her new career, like many of that company's ageing acquisitions, was relatively short and she was scrapped at Gadani Beach in 1977. P.H.B.

PEARL ASIA 1957 8,000 grt. Good Hope Shipping Co. Ltd.

31.10.71

The railway network in the north-west was already well established when the Manchester Ship Canal was constructed at the end of the 19th century and substantial bridges and earthworks were required to raise those lines where they crossed the course of the Canal. Latchford Viaduct, to the east of Warrington, carrying the now closed and lifted section of the Timperley – Garston line (through Warrington Arpley), is one of four similar structures on the Canal and it provides an impressive frame as the bulk carrier Pearl Asia *slows to enter Latchford Locks, just visible ahead. The height of these viaducts was just over 72'*

(22m) above water level, this dimension having been determined by the London & North Western Railway Company's viaduct at Runcorn, constructed in 1868 to conform with the requirements of what was then a navigable stretch of the Mersey. The Pearl Asia *may be better remembered as the* Crystal Crown, *one of six similar vessels built in the fifties for the Sugar Line, a subsidiary of United Molasses. Designed principally for the carriage of raw sugar to the refineries, they were frequently engaged in other bulk trades.* P.H.B.

15

SCHOLAR 1965 7,606 grt. T. & J. Harrison Ltd.

Catching the last of the evening sunlight, the Scholar *gets underway down Eastham Channel after discharging her cargo at Manchester Docks. Originally built as the* Samaria *for the North Atlantic services of Cunard Line, she was acquired by Harrison's in 1969, together with a sistership, the* Scythia, *which became the* Merchant, *when they were prematurely displaced by the onslaught of containerisation. Together with a third sister the* Scotia, *these had been built by Cammell Laird for bareboat charter to Cunard by the actual owners, North Western Line Mersey Ltd., a subsidiary of the builders. Harrison*

10.5.72

employed them principally upon their services to the Caribbean until once again the advent of container ships was to bring about their demise ten years later. The pair were sold in 1979 to Greek flagged companies controlled by the Liberian based Manta Shipping Co. and both were to have untimely ends. Just over a year later the Steel Trader *(ex* Scholar*) was trapped at Khorramshahr and became a gutted victim of the Iran – Iraq war. In 1984 the* Sisal Trader *(ex* Merchant*) was driven aground off Madagascar and, although subsequently salved, was sold to Pakistani breakers.*

P.H.B.

16

MARKHOR 1963 9,120 grt. Cunard Brocklebank Ltd.

June 80

T. & J. Brocklebank Ltd., could trace its origins back to 1770 and, with some justification, claim to be the oldest established British Shipping company. Controlled by the Cunard Steamship Co., for many years, Brocklebank's latterly became an ever more integral part of that organisation, but none the less retained its colours and traditional Indian names. By the time this photograph was taken their fleet had been reduced to just three vessels of which the Markhor, seen here turning off Gladstone Locks outward bound, was the only

one to have actually been built for the company. However, some years previously her ownership had passed to Eggar, Forrester (Holdings) Ltd. and bareboat chartered back in an arrangement that became increasingly common with British shipping concerns. The following year the Markhor was sold, becoming the Kara Unicorn under the Liberian flag and passed to Chinese breakers in 1984.

P.H.B.

HECTOR   1950   9,781 grt.   Blue Funnel Line Ltd.

The carefully proportioned lines and distinctive perpendicular profiles lent the vessels of Alfred Holt's Blue Funnel Line a particular distinction which, reinforced with the upright light blue funnels and Homeric names from Greek mythology, gave the company, to use a modern idiom, a strong corporate image. The Hector, built by Harland & Wolff at Belfast, was one of four particularly fine steam turbine powered cargo liners employed on the U.K. – Australia service and the classic Blue Funnel lines are seen here to advantage as she heads out down the Crosby Channel in gale conditions. Originally provided with

29.6.70

facilities for 30 First Class passengers, the vessels were transferred to the Far Eastern trades in the late sixties by which time the carriage of passengers had been discontinued, and one of the original three pairs of lifeboats removed. Soaring fuel prices hastened the demise of the oil burning steamers and in 1972 the Hector ended her days, like so many other British vessels of that time, in a breakers yard at Kaohsiung.

P.H.B.

PHILOCTETES   1950   9.754 grt.   Blue Funnel Line Ltd.

30.11.72

Philoctetes, the bowman from the Isle of Lemnos, in avenging the death of Achilles, came to prominence in the final stages of the siege of Troy. It was, therefore, fitting that this Greek hero should have been chosen when the last of the "P" Class cargo liners was renamed shortly before withdrawal. Better known as the Patroclus for the previous 22 years of service, she was one of what were perhaps the finest of the post-war Blue Funnel designs. Together with the slightly larger "H" class, they were at the time of building the most powerful single-screw turbine powered ships and were credited with a service speed of 18 knots. *Disposal of the steamers came during 1972 with the four "Priam" class ships of the associated Glen Lines being transferred to the parent company as replacements. Names in line with the other members of this class already in the fleet were chosen, and thus the Patroclus released the title to her successor, assuming her new identity as she loaded her final cargo. With a night-time departure anticipated, advantage was taken of the illumination from the Clan Line quay opposite to record this reflective evening view in Vittoria Dock.*

P.H.B.   **19**

ELPENOR   1954   7,425 grt.   Blue Funnel Line

9.5.72

The Anchises or "A" class comprised the largest type numerically within the Blue Funnel fleet and in the eleven years from the delivery of the lead ship in 1947, no fewer than 27 examples were built to the same basic design. Improvements and modifications were incorporated as the construction programme progressed, in particular developments in the main engine installations, and the class was sub-divided by the company into 6 groups. The Elpenor was from the fourth group, designated Mark A4 which, with the early disposal of the later Marks A5/6 to Somali flagged Chinese interests in 1972, were the last of the class to remain in service.

In 1972 the Far Eastern service had yet to feel the full force of containerisation and there were few times when there was not at least one of the class loading in Vittoria Dock or the adjacent Cathcart St. berth in the East Float. At the beginning of another lengthy voyage that would take her via the Cape to Penang, Port Kelang, Singapore, Bangkok and on to Manila, the Elpenor was in pristine condition as she gets under way off Alfred Locks. Sold in 1977 to the Gulf Shipping group, she joined many of her former compatriots sold to this concern. As the United Concord she survived for a further two years before making the inevitable trip to the breakers at Kaohsiung.

P.H.B.

AMARNA   1949   3,422 grt.   Moss-Hutchison Line Ltd.

28.2.75

The Moss-Hutchison Line had a long association with Liverpool dating from the formation of James Moss's shipping company in the early part of the last century. Although acquired by the P. & O. group in 1935, the line retained its identity until the last two of its vessels were sold off in 1979. The Amarna was one of seven similar well proportioned motorships that were delivered between 1947-52. Generally employed on the Moss-Hutchison service from Liverpool to Mediterranean ports, for one year from 1967, the Amarna was chartered by Cunard for their Great Lakes service and renamed Assyria for the duration. One of the last of this group to be withdrawn, she was sold in 1975 to the Grecomar Shipping Agency who ultimately purchased all seven of these vessels. (They also acquired about this time the two Blue Funnel ships that had been trapped in the Suez Canal). Renamed Kastriani III, she retained her association with the Mediterranean, trading principally between Egypt and the Black Sea until sold in 1982. Thereafter she languished at Aden and although reported to be renamed Montrose by her new Gibraltar flag owners, it would seem that this change was not effected and over a year later she arrived at Gadani Beach in Pakistan for scrapping in 1984.

P.H.B.

TOWNSVILLE STAR   1957   10,632 grt.   Blue Star Line Ltd.

The summer of 1975 was exceptionally fine and conditions on this early July morning can hardly have been better than for the arrival of the Townsville Star, seen here stemming the ebb tide off Gladstone Lock. Ostensibly a Blue Star ship, the Townsville Star was one of several within the Vestey group to be registered in the ownership of Salient Shipping Co., a Bermudan based subsidiary. Intially registered in the island's principal port, Hamilton, only a year later this was changed to London, in line with the rest of the parent fleet. She, and her sistership the Gladstone Star, were built by Bremer Vulkan at Vegesack on the

Weser, who the previous year had completed an order for three slightly smaller near sisterships. For most of her service the Townsville Star carried the Blue Star colours on her prominent funnel, but for a while ran with those of Crusader Shipping, a consortium of British Conference Lines, including Blue Star, established to develop their Pacific Ocean services. She was one of the last conventional Blue Star vessels to serve the port until withdrawn and sold to Taiwanese breakers in 1980.

P.H.B.

CITY OF RIPON   1956   7,713 grt.   Ellerman Lines Ltd.

The City Line was one of the principal constituents of Ellerman Lines, an amalgam of companies created by John Reeves Ellerman in the early years of this century. Their City nomenclature was eventually applied to the majority of vessels taken into the combined fleet. The Ellerman funnel markings, first introduced in 1904, were derived from those of Liverpool's Alexandra Towing Co., – with their approval – differing only in the omission of the narrow black band separating the white from the buff base. Each of the companies did, however, retain their own houseflag, and port of registry, up until 1973 when most of the vessels still then remaining were brought under the common ownership of Ellerman Lines Ltd.

Having suffered massive wartime losses, Ellerman's invested heavily in their reconstruction programme, placing orders for large groups of vessels which were allocated throughout their fleet. The City of Ripon was one of six similar motorships completed in the mid-fifties, two of which were placed in the ownership of City Line. These vessels had a substantial appearance, with the tall funnel emphasising the rather stern profile. An unusual feature was the provision of portholes, rather than windows, in the superstructure front, a practice more often associated with Japanese shipyards. In 1978 the City of Ripon was sold to Ben Line and renamed Benvannoch, but less than twelve months later was despatched to breakers at Taiwan.

P.H.B.

LALANDE   1940   6,902 grt.   Lamport & Holt Ltd.

The Lalande had originally entered service as the Empire Voice, *one of the many "Empire" ships built to government order during the war and placed under the management of established shipping concerns. With simplicity the order of the day at that time, her machinery was surprisingly complex with a low pressure exhaust turbine hydraulically coupled to the single shaft driven by the ubiquitous triple expansion steam engine. Booth Line, her wartime managers, acquired her on release from Ministry service in 1946. As the* Bernard, *she was placed on their Amazon service but the following year was transferred to Lamport & Holt, both companies being by then part of the Vestey group. Lamport's traditionally named their ships after artists, authors and poets and initially she became the* Byron *with the renaming to* Lalande *coming in 1953. One can only muse at this juncture over the reason why an 18th century French astronomer should have been favoured in place of one of the greatest British literary figures. Sold in 1961, she was renamed* Uncle Bart *for the delivery voyage to Japanese breakers.*

It is interesting to note that construction work was still in hand in this 1959 view in Canada Dock with the warehouses yet to be erected. These were demolished some years ago and the quayside is now piled high with scrap for export.

23.7.59

H.B. Christiansen

BENARKLE 1946 9,868 grt. The Ben Line Steamers Ltd.

18.3.72

As the pressures during the early phase of the war to replace the heavy losses with speedily built and necessarily utilitarian tonnage eased, the Government turned its attention to producing a superior design suitable for peacetime trading. The "Standard Fast" type emerged in 1943 and although only fourteen of these entered service with Empire names under Ministry ownership, the design, with various modifications, was adopted by a number of liner companies to help rebuild their post-war fleets. Ellerman Lines took six of these into their fleet, with four flying the houseflag of its Hall Line.

Three of these passed to Ben Line in 1968 including the Swan Hunter built City of Poona *which became their* Benarkle. *In Ellerman colours she had been a regular trader to the Mersey on the East African and Indian services. Although Ben Line vessels made only occasional calls at the Port, this was the first of two visits the* Benarkle *was to make in 1972. She is seen here passing through Langton Dock under tow to her berth in the adjacent Canada Dock.*

P.H.B.

IKEJA PALM 1961 5,682 grt. Palm Line Ltd

16.8.81

Aesthetics were still a matter worthy of consideration in 1961, at least so far as Palm Line and Swan Hunter, the builders of the Ikeja Palm, were concerned. It would certainly have been difficult to have improved on the lines or the balance of this workaday cargo ship and sadly, as the decade advanced, many of the established principles of good design were abandoned, leading inexorably to the cumbersome and ill proportioned profiles that increasingly disgrace the seas today. The funnel markings were a particularly attractive feature of the Palm Line vessels, although surprisingly these were not well received when the company was born out of the United Africa Co., in 1949. Both these companies were subsidiaries of the international Unilever Group, whose British manufacturing interests are centred on Merseyside and, up to 1956, their ships were managed from and registered at Liverpool. The Ikeja Palm and the generally similar but slightly larger Lagos Palm, delivered some weeks later, were the last traditional freighters to be built for Palm Line. Their fleet then stood at a peak of 24 vessels but thereafter came the inevitable period of decline with the last vessel being sold in 1985. The title and trading rights of the company were acquired by Elder Dempster the following year, who too in turn, only a few years later, had disposed of their fleet when it was bought out by the French Delmas-Vieljeux company.

P.H.B.

DONGA   1960   6,565 grt   Elder Dempster Lines Ltd.

One of the three sisterships – the other two being Dalla and Dumbaia – the Donga was built by Lithgows Ltd of Port Glasgow for Henderson's British & Burmese S.N.Co. Ltd., and thus her port of registry was Glasgow. As her West African name suggests, however, this vessel was employed on Elder Dempster Line services, rather than those of her registered owners to Burma. Despite her by then somewhat rundown condition, she looks particularly fine in Elder's colours, all the more so as the white paint had been re-instated to the fo'c'sle and poop for the last few years of the company's conventional liner services.

Although lightly laden off the entrance to Liverpool's Langton Lock, Donga has arrived from a foreign port, as denoted by the yellow 'Q' flag flying from her signal mast – indicating that she is requiring 'free pratique' (i.e. health clearance) from HM Customs & Excise. Sold to Greeks in March 1981, she was given the name Diamant Merchant. It was reported that there had been a transfer to the Cypriot flag the following year under the new name of Lydra, however this proved to be erroneous, as it was under her Greek identity that she was delivered to Port Alang in India on 7th October 1983 for demolition.   N.P.B.

27

ROMNEY 1952 8,138 grt. Lamport & Holt Line Ltd.

5.12.76

A cold and frosty Saturday morning, as this classic British steam turbine freighter leaves the Ship Canal 80 ft entrance lock after an overnight passage down from Manchester, to enter the Mersey's Eastham Channel, under the guidance of a single head tug provided by the Alexandra Towing Co., Ltd. Named after the 18th century English painter, George Romney, this vessel was to give her Liverpool owners 26 years of service following her
delivery in May 1952 as the fleet's flagship from the Mersey's own shipyard of Cammell Laird & Co., Ltd. Her final voyage took her from the Mersey on October 2nd 1978 to the breakers yard of Shipbreaking Industries Ltd., at Faslane in Scotland, where she arrived the following day. She was the last steam ship in the Lamport fleet.

N.P.B.

SUEVIC 1950 13,350 grt. Shaw Savill & Albion Co. Ltd.

28.4.73

Prior to becoming part of the Furness Withy Group in the 1930's, Shaw Savill had been associated with the White Star Line whose funnel colours and naming policy they perpetuated following the merger of that company with Cunard after the collapse of Lord Kylsant's shipping empire. The Suevic was one of three sister ships which, despite their substantial superstructure, did not carry passengers. The superbly well balanced profile was marred only by the omission of a mainmast, the provision of which distinguished the Persic, the first of the trio to enter service. Apart from a fire in 1968, the Suevic seems to have had a fairly uneventful career, unlike the third sister Runic which became a total loss in 1961 after striking a reef off the Australian coast. Interestingly it was the Suevic of a like named pair of White Star liners that suffered a similar fate off the Irish coast in 1907. She was, however, to be more fortunate and, following the salvage of the after part, she was returned to service with a new bow section.

This 1973 view is from the New Brighton foreshore as the Suevic, nearing the end of her service, sails up the Crosby Channel at low water. The following year she was sold to Taiwanese breakers.

P.H.B.

TANGISTAN   1950   7,222 grt.   Strick Line Ltd.

1.1.71

New Year's Day 1971 was gloriously sunny throughout, providing perfect conditions to record the arrival of Strick Lines Tangistan at Eastham. In conjunction with Ellerman Lines, Strick operated a joint service to Red Sea Ports and the Tangistan would probably have been bringing in a cargo including cotton for discharge at Manchester, having already called at Emden and Glasgow on this voyage. The distinctive Strick funnel markings were, *unfortunately, to disappear two years later, along with those of the majority of companies within the P. & O. Group when their vessels were integrated into the General Cargo Division and re-painted in the new corporate livery. The Tangistan was to retain her traditional colours to the end, however, with her withdrawal and scrapping coming just over twelve months after the date of this photograph.*

P.H.B.

27.7.75

STRATHASLAK   1960   9,423 grt.   P. & O. S.N. Co.

The new P. & O. colour scheme, as originally applied to the cargo vessels, was rather drab and uninspiring. The plain black hull with dark red boot-topping, cream masts and the light blue funnel carrying the white P. & O. shadow logo seemed a poor replacement for the splendid and distinctive colours that they had supplanted. The adoption some time later of corn yellow hulls with contrasting blue boot-topping was a welcome improvement and is seen to good effect on the **Strathaslak**, *formerly the* **Kohistan** *of Strick Lines, as she gets underway in the river after dropping off the tug that had escorted her out of Langton Lock.*

Whilst P. & O. is perhaps not a company that would immediately be associated with Merseyside, its extensive shipping empire embraced a considerable number of concerns that had for many years retained their own identities. On the formation of their General Cargo Division in 1971, over 100 conventional cargo ships in the ownership of ten different companies came under their auspices many, such as those of the Federal, Hain-Nourse, Moss Hutchinson and Strick Companies, regularly trading to the port.

P.H.B.

HINAKURA   1949   11,272 grt   Federal Steam Nav. Co. Ltd.

The origins of the Federal houseflag, proudly displayed on their black topped deep red funnels, has been told before but is none the less worth recounting here. Money Wigram, the ancestor of the company, had, as its houseflag, the red cross of St. George on a white ground. When one of their sailing ships ventured into sight of the Portsmouth naval base, an Admiral took offence at it flying what could be confused with the flag of the Navy's Commander-in-Chief. The matter was speedily rectified by attaching a rectangle of blue cloth to the centre of the red cross. Honour was restored; the design immortalised. Sadly these fine funnel colours were amongst those to fall victim to the P. & O. reorganisation in the 1970's. Whilst the older vessels adopted the new livery in 1973, for some reason the newer reefer vessels retained the traditional colours until 1976, albeit in combination with a garish and ill-matched light green hull of sickly hue.

The Federal S.N. Co. had been absorbed by the New Zealand Shg. Co. in 1913 and the two companies remained closely linked following their takeover by P. & O. in 1916. Until 1966 both retained their own identities but in that year the New Zealand vessels , including the Hinakura, were transferred to Federal ownership and adopted their colours. The Hinakura was one of a class of eight twin-screw refrigerated motorships divided between the two companies and was to give her owners a creditable 25 years of service before withdrawal in 1974.

P.H.B.

NICOLAS BOWATER   1958   6,875 grt.   Bowater S.S. Co. Ltd.

16.7.72

*The Bowater Paper Corporation, through its shipping subsidiary, owned a number of very smart freighters to serve their facilities and these were regular visitors to their mill at Ellesmere Port, now the premises of the Bridgewater Paper Co. Ltd. Nicolas Bowater was the company's flagship and was a slightly larger version of two earlier sisterships which were also products of the Dumbarton Yard of Wm. Denny & Bros. Ltd. All three were powered by steam turbines and like all the fleet were heavily built ships, strengthened for navigation in ice. The company had an attractive livery, with the pale cream upperworks nicely complimenting the brunswick green hull and this was generally kept in exemplary condition. Even the cream paintwork has been carried into the anchor recess. By the time of this photograph the original light green boot-topping had been replaced by the more functional, dull red colour. During the 1970's the fleet was gradually run down with the **Nicolas Bowater** being sold to Liberian owners in 1973, and re-named **Vall Comet**. In company with many steamships at that time she had a relatively short life and was scrapped in 1977.*

P.H.B.

33

I CONGRESO DEL PARTIDO   1975,   9,328 grt.   Empresa De Navegacion Mambisa

1.3.86

The SD14 design was one of the great, and far too few, success stories of British shipbuilding. It emerged as one of the so called "Liberty Ship Replacement" types with the first example, the Nicola, being delivered to Greek owners in 1968. Over the next 20 years no fewer than 211 SD14's were constructed, not only by Austin & Pickersgill and their associated companies, but also by licensees in Brazil and Greece. The original concept of a minimal cost, basic shelter deck freighter soon changed as liner operators began to take an interest in the design and ever more sophisticated variants were produced, especially in the type of cargo handling gear fitted. The Cubans in particular favoured the SD14 and having had five examples built to their own account, subsequently acquired many more but placed these under the various ownership and flag identities. The I Congreso Del Partido was one of those operated directly by the state shipping company and she had brought in a cargo of animal feedstuffs, one of the last bulk cargoes still conveyed in general cargo vessels. This stern view of her sailing highlights the distinctive features, notably the ribbed superstructure plating, of these ships.

34

P.H.B.

BALASHOV   1955   3,258 grt.   USSR Latvian Shipping Co.

4.10.78

A four hatched Russian steamer, propelled by a 4 cylinder compound reciprocating engine with a low pressure exhaust turbine. By the time this photo was taken, this was a type of vessel that oozed character from every seam and unfortunately, from the observers point of view, was becoming increasingly rare. Built by the East German Schiffswerft Neptun yard at Rostock as one of a class of 30 ships, known as the 'Kolomna' type – 9 of them went into Russian naval service as depot ships.   Their design concept owed something to the wartime 'Scandinavian' design built in British yards and the German Hansa 'A' and Hansa 'B' types. The starboard lifeboat on the superstructure appears to be a modern fibreglass replacement. Seen here off Eastham Ferry prior to locking into the Manchester Ship Canal, the Balashov survived until 10/9/85 when she arrived at Aviles in Spain for scrap.

N.P.B.

CLYDE ORE   1960   9,156 grt.   Ore Carriers of Liberia Inc.

31.5.75

It is particularly clear May day, and the North Westerly winds have blown away all traces of haze and mist to reveal Winter Hill, near Horwich, 25 miles distant across the Lancashire plain as the Clyde Ore ploughs down the Crosby Channel outward bound in ballast from Birkenhead. Although operating under the Liberian flag, this vessel along with a number of sisters all originating from the Hamburg shipyard of Schlieker Werft and featuring names of British and German rivers, were actually German owned, and on long term charter to the British Steel Corporation.   Their inward cargoes of iron ore were

discharged at Birkenhead's Bidston Dock for onward rail transport to the Shotton Steelworks on Deeside. When new, these vessels sported grey hulls, but in the last year or two of their charters, these were repainted black, and in some cases transferred to the Greek Flag without change of name. Clyde Ore was actually sold late in 1975 to become the Garden Saturn under Greek registry. However, in December 1976 she was laid up in Piraeus, eventually being despatched in July 1978 to Spain for demolition at Gandia.

N.P.B.

ARISAIG   1957   6,872 grt.   Scottish Ore Carriers Ltd.   J. & J. Denholm (Management) Ltd.

15.5.71

The Glasgow Shipowners and Managers J. & J. Denholm Ltd., through a number of its subsidiaries, had interests in several of the ore carriers built in the 1950's for long term charter to the British Iron & Steel Corp. Scottish Ore Carriers was a joint venture with the Clydeside shipbuilders Lithgows Ltd., who produced a series of 4 ships of limited dimensions that enabled them to serve the restricted port facilities at Workington and Port Talbot. They were also well suited to the transit of the Manchester Ship Canal and often brought in cargoes for the furnaces of the Lancashire Steel Co., at Irlam. The Arisaig was the third of the original quartet which, whilst of very similar external appearance, had an amazing variety of machinery installations. A motorship, she was possibly the least interesting mechanically of the group, whereas the Morar of 1958 had, most unusually, a free piston gas turbine installation. The remaining pair were powered by the more traditional, if by then somewhat outdated, triple expansion steam reciprocating engines. All were to have comparatively short careers and by 1971 only the Arisaig remained of these four vessels. She too was disposed of the following year and was cut up at Faslane on the river she had entered service on only 15 years before.

P.H.B.

37

BRITISH RELIANCE   1950   11,026 grt.   B.P. Tanker Co. Ltd.

Although British Petroleum operated a substantial fleet of tankers, they called relatively infrequently on the river and this visit of the then 22 year old British Reliance was something of a rarity. Her arrival came in the aftermath of a summer evening storm and the river is bathed in an ethereal blue light as she makes her way past Seacombe. Just visible behind, at the Salisbury Dock entrance, is Jesse Hartley's notable five-faced Victoria clock tower, built in 1848. The British Reliance would be bringing in a cargo of refined product, possibly Naphtha, from B.P.'s South Wales refinery, which she discharged at the Dingle Tanker Buoy. This mid-river mooring facility replaced the old jetties serving the Dingle Tank farm which was closed and swept away not many years after, with the site later developed as part of the Liverpool Garden Festival. One of a series of 20 similar tankers, the British Reliance was involved in a collision with a Swedish freighter later that year and was sold some months after. As the Bangor Bay, and later the Greek flagged Ocean Princess, she traded until 1975 when she was scrapped in Spain.

P.H.B.

CINULIA 1955 9.094 grt. Shell Tankers N.V.

Along with her two sisters Camitia *and* Crania, *these Dutch flag Shell motor tankers were regular visitors to the Manchester Ship Canal, often bringing in cargoes of base lubricants for the company's Stanlow Refinery or the grease plant up at Barton near Manchester. Note that the top masts have been struck in readiness for passage along the upper reaches. The trio had particularly long lives,* Cinulia, *the last survivor managing 31 years*

30.1.80

before going to the breakers at Selang in Indonesia where she arrived 4/7/86. Here, the Cinulia *which was built by P. Smit Jnr., of Rotterdam, has just entered the Eastham Channel off Bromborough. Interestingly, she still retains the raised 'scallop' motif on the funnel – most of the fleet by this time merely had the device painted on.*

N.P.B.

LUGANO   1949   2,925 grt.   Cia. Nav. Rivabella S.A.

7.10.72

Making what was possibly her first, but most certainly her last, visit to the port was the former East Coast Collier Hudson Firth. Built in 1949 by the Ailsa S.B. Co. Ltd. at Troon for the Hudson S.S. Co. Ltd., she passed to Panamanian owners in 1967 who traded her as the Lugano for a further five years. Having discharged her final cargo at Birkenhead, she lay over on Cavendish Quay in the west float during the weekend and departed for the breakers yard of W.H. Arnott Young at Dalmuir on the Clyde, later in the following week. The Spiller's and Rank's Ocean Flour Mills, referred to on page 10, both levelled some years ago, can be seen in the background, left.

P.H.B.

BEN VEG   1965   346 grt.   Ramsey Steamship Co. Ltd.

14.3.77

Originally developed by the St. Helens Railway Company, predominantly for the purpose of exporting coal from the South Lancashire coalfields, each of the three docks comprising the Garston system – namely, North, Old and Stalbridge were equipped with a variety of rail connected coal drops for loading vessels. By the time this photo was taken only 4 of the original 12 were in service. Ben Veg is loading coal in the Old Dock. Note the 16 ton mineral wagon in the process of depositing its load through the end door – the white diagonal stripe on the wagon indicating to the shunters which end was so equipped. The vessel is using its port anchor and fo'c'sle winch to move along the quayside in order to *obtain an even distribution of the cargo. Built in Holland, as indicated by the acorns on the mastheads, her name translated from the Manx Gaelic means 'Little Woman'. She remained with Ramsey Steam until 1979, when she passed through the hands of a number of UK owners without change of name until becoming The Benn in 1980 under the St. Vincent flag. Renamed Benn in 1984 without change of ownership, she eventually disappeared without trace in January 1991, whilst being towed from Port of Spain to Castries in bad weather.*

N.P.B.

KINGSNORTH FISHER 1966 2,355 grt. James Fisher & Sons Ltd.

29.10.83

Outward bound from the Manchester Ship Canal at Bromborough is the Kingsnorth Fisher. She was built by Hall, Russell & Co Ltd., Aberdeen, and is one of a pair of diesel electric engined heavy lift vessels – the other being Aberthaw Fisher – completed for long term charter to the Central Electricity Generating Board (whose insignia can be seen front of the superstructure). They were designed principally to carry large and heavy machinery to power station sites where access or lifting equipment was restricted. Both vessels were – and in fact still are – regular visitors to the Manchester Ship Canal, where they had an appropriated berth with its own ro ro ramp in Manchester's Pomona Dock No. 2.

They were the last commercial vessels to trade into the Pomona Docks, and upon final closure of this system, the loading berth was moved further down the Canal to the North Wall at Ellesmere Port. In 1990, upon privatisation of the electricity supply industry, the charter passed to National Power PLC, with a resultant change of name for this vessel to New Generation. She can be distinguished from her Troon built sistership – now renamed National Generation by the SATCOM dome that has now been fitted atop the wheelhouse.

N.P.B.

SANGUITY 1956 1,543 grt. F.T. Everard & Sons Ltd.

27.1.71

F.T. Everard have long been a dominant force in coastal shipping, operating a sizable fleet of both dry-cargo vessels and tankers which, even by the early seventies, still comprised over fifty craft. In more recent years, whilst the number of vessels has decreased considerably, the company is still one of the largest privately owned short sea operators under the British flag. The Sanguity *was one of a class of 10 similar ships of the traditional 3 island configuration with raised quarterdeck that entered service over a period between 1949 and 1958. They introduced the smart yellow hull and funnel colours into the fleet,* *which were subsequently adopted for all the larger dry-cargo ships. Sold in 1978 to a Panamanian concern, she was renamed* **Ramona** *and at the time of writing she had been laying at Idefjord, just south of Oslo, since July 1986 and would seem unlikely to trade again.*

Another Eastham view, this was one of those rare occasions when the sun broke through an otherwise overcast sky at just the right time

P.H.B.   **43**

RAMSEY   1965   446 grt.   Isle of Man Steam Packet Co. Ltd.

26.9.72

Here seen leaving Langton Lock, with a deck cargo of pre-fabricated wooden roof trusses loaded at East Hornby Dock, Ramsey *was the last conventional cargo vessel built for the company. She was delivered by the Ailsa Shipbuilding Company at Troon, and was a replacement for the 1921 steamer* Conister. *Her size allowed her to serve her namesake port as well as the island's capital, Douglas. Prior to 1972, the Steam Packet's freighters used an allocated berth in the Coburg Dock, in Liverpool's south docks system. The switch to Hornby Dock in the North was soon followed by a change over from break bulk to unitised cargo. Unfortunately, the* Ramsey *was not considered suitable for conversion to this mode of operation, and was sold in 1973, becoming the* Hoofort *under the UK flag. Ironically, she was replaced by the second* Conister – *a second hand purchase, which had already undergone conversion for container traffic. The* Ramsey *remains in service today as the* Arquipelago *under the Cape Verde Islands flag, having also born the name* Boa Entrado *between 1982 and 1990. Note that on the voyage depicted above, the master has a Mersey Pilotage exemption certificate as indicated by the flying of the red and white pilotage licence flag – the flag 'H' from the International Code of Signals – turned through 90 degrees.*

P.H.B.

31.8.81

ASSIDUITY 1964 1,249 grt. F.T. Everard & Sons Ltd.

Although a London firm, members of the Everard fleet were regular visitors to the Mersey, and at one stage, the company maintained an agency office at Bromborough Dock. This **Assiduity** *(the second in the fleet to bear the name), was a coastal tanker built by the Goole Shipbuilding & Repairing Co., Ltd., at Goole. Originally designed for East Coast UK service from Mobil's Coryton Refinery on the Lower Thames, she was not found to be entirely satisfactory for the work and was eventually replaced by the same company's* **Audacity.** *Re-engined in 1973,* **Assiduity** *continued in Everard's service on hydro-*

carbon oils work until sold to Greek buyers in 1984. She was then renamed Vasiliki V (translated as **Queen V***), the purchasers being active in buying former British coastal tankers, upon which they proceeded to bestow the same name, merely differentiating by a different Roman numeric suffix. In this view on the approach to Eastham Ferry,* **Assiduity** *is inward bound in ballast for the Manchester Ship Canal.*

N.P.B.

45

1.7.81

TOPAZ   1962   1,597 grt.   Stephenson Clarke Shipping Ltd.

Originally built for William Robertson's Gem Line Ltd., of Glasgow by the Ailsa Shipbuilding Co., Ltd., of Troon, Topaz and her slightly younger sister ship Tourmaline were frequent visitors to Mersey ports. One of the regular cargoes carried was silversand from Antwerp for the St. Helens glass industry, which was discharged at Liverpool's East Bramley-Moore dock, and latterly at Runcorn. In 1970, Gem Line was acquired by the Powell Duffryn group, although it maintained its separate identity until 1978 when it was eventually integrated with their Stephenson Clarke fleet. It is in the latter company's colours that the vessel is illustrated above, whilst on passage down the Manchester Ship Canal at Ince Low Cutting; her original funnel colours being plain black. The interesting little craft being overtaken is the Manchester Ship Canal's pay boat which distributed wages to employees working afloat up and down the Canal. Topaz was sold out of the fleet in 1982, and is currently operating under the Maltese flag as Sorocco, having during the years 1982 to 1990 also carried the names Proba, Fergus H, and Socotra.

46

N.P.B.

15.5.66

ULSTER MONARCH   1929   3,815 grt.   Belfast S.S. Co. Ltd.

The Ulster Monarch was the first of 12 "Seaway" class ferries to be built by Harland & Wolff at Belfast for the Irish services of companies within the Coast Lines group. Requisitioned shortly after the outbreak of war, together with her two sisterships in the Belfast Steamship Company's fleet, she had a distinguished career, later as H.M.S. Ulster Monarch, which saw her participating in actions throughout Europe and Africa, including a circumnavigation of the continent. In 1946 she returned to service on the Liverpool – Belfast overnight sailings, the only survivor of the original trio. A major refit followed in

1950 when the two flat topped funnels, which so typified Harland & Wolff motorships of that period, were replaced with a more rakish pair. Her final voyage came in October 1966 and she was later sold to Belgian breakers at Ghent.

With their evening departures and early morning arrivals, recording the Irish ferries was not easy and the photographer took advantage of the temporary closure of the Waterloo lock entrance which resulted in a later docking via Langton Lock to record this beautiful study shortly before she was withdrawn.

M. McRonald

47

ULSTER PRINCE 1967 4,270 grt. Belfast S.S. Co., Ltd.

12.9.75

The two car ferries that entered service on the Liverpool – Belfast route in 1967 were, most appropriately, products of the shipyards on the rivers they served. The Ulster Prince came from the Queen's Island yard of Harland & Wolff Ltd., and the Ulster Queen from Cammell Laird & Co. Like the passenger only ferries they replaced, the pair led a leisurely nocturnal existence, each making only six single overnight crossings a week, laying by on their berths for the rest of the day. A return daylight crossing was introduced for a short period, enabling this late afternoon arrival to be recorded. Occasionally passages were also made between booked sailings, conveying troops to and from Northern Ireland. Following the takeover of the Coast Lines group in 1971 by P. & O., their influence

gradually manifested itself, culminating in the pale blue and white colours of their Short Sea Shipping division, replacing those of the Belfast company in 1978. Around the same time P. & O. became the registered owners of the two vessels. The design of these ferries was restrictive, both in the number and size of vehicles that could be carried, with the problem exacerbated by the stern only loading arrangements. Their withdrawal in 1981, after mounting losses on the route, was not, therefore, surprising and the following year both were sold to Cypriot flag buyers. The Ulster Prince became the Lady M, but two years later changed hands again, taking the name Tangpakorn as which she passed to China Ocean Shipping Co. and is believed to be still in service.

P.H.B.

MUNSTER 1948 4,142 grt. British & Irish Steam Packet Co. Ltd.

The Leinster *and* Munster, *which entered service on the Liverpool – Dublin route in 1948, were replacements for two pre-war ships of the same names; the* Leinster *of 1937 having been transferred in 1945 to the Belfast run and the* Munster *having been lost in 1940. They were near identical sisterships to their predecessors, all being developments of the "Seaway" type introduced with the* Ulster Monarch *(q.v.) Then an Irish flagged subsidiary of Coast Lines, the attractive livery of the B. & I. line, nicely adopting the colours of the Irish Tricolour, has rarely been bettered. As with the* Ulster Monarch, *the temporary diversion via Langton Lock provided a perfect opportunity for this early morning*

photograph. In 1965 Coast Lines sold B. & I. to the Irish Government to assist in the financing of two new car ferries for the Belfast service. Under its new mangement the fleet was repainted in a more mundane, predominantly black and white colour scheme that did little to enhance these elegant ships. The pair were soon to be replaced, however, by car ferries with the Munster, *the first to be sold in 1968, passing to the Greek Epirotiki organisation. As the* Orpheus, *and still recognisable from her Irish Sea days, she is still engaged in cruising, principally in the Mediterranean, although on at least two occasions she has returned to British waters.*

M. McRonald

LADY OF MANN   1930   3,104 grt.   Isle of Man Steam Packet Co. Ltd.

The Lady of Mann was a special ship in many ways and there can have been few steamers that have endeared themselves as much to both crew and traveller alike. Ordered during the depths of the depression, the excellence of her construction was a tribute to the skill of the senior personnel retained by the builders during those dire times. She was launched from the Barrow-in-Furness yard of Vickers Armstrong in March 1930 by the Duchess of Atholl whose husband's ancestors had earlier held the title Lord of Mann. Often referred to as the company's centenary ship, the "Lady" was the largest steamer to be built for them and on trials attained a speed of nearly 23 knots. Designed principally for the

Douglas – Fleetwood service, in 1933 she adopted the white livery with green boot-topping pioneered by the Ben-my-Chree the previous year. War-time service in a less fetching overall grey took both these vessels well beyond the confines of the Irish Sea and her sea-going capabilities were severely tested in Atlantic passages to Iceland and the Faroes. A long and glorious post-war service finally ended towards the close of the 1971 season. Although there was talk at the time of preservation for the planned Maritime Museum, after a period of lay-up at Barrow, she left in tow shortly after Christmas bound for demolition at Dalmuir on the Clyde.

M. McRonald

MANXMAN 1955 2,495 grt. Isle of Man Steam Packet Co. Ltd.

22.6.80

The Manxman was the last of a series of six elegant twin-screw steamers built by Cammell Laird & Co. Ltd. between 1946-55 for the Isle of Man Steam Packet Co Ltd. Each differed slightly in external detail, with the Manxman carrying two of her three pairs of lifeboats on gravity davits, clear of the decks. She was also the only one of the group to have double reduction gearing to the turbines, which were driven by superheated steam. After the 1980 season, only the Manxman remained of the passenger only ferries and she attained something of a celebrity status during the final two years of her career, in which she took the last of the company's sailings from Douglas to Llandudno. On withdrawal at the end of the 1982 season she was sold to buyers who took her to the old Preston Docks as the centrepiece of a new leisure development. In 1990 she returned to Liverpool, in tow, where she remains in use as a night-club, berthed in Waterloo Dock, coincidentally directly behind her stern on this view. Unfortunately, she has not been retained in the Steam Packet's colours.

As many would prefer to remember the last of the classic Manx steamers, the Manxman gives two blasts on the distinctive triple-chime whistle announcing her turn to port to bring her alongside the Prince's landing stage with the return sailing from Llandudno. P.H.B.

May Day 1977 in the Crosby Channel.

1.5.77

The initial cruise of a week's programme for the paddle steamer Waverley saw her on a well supported Liverpool – Llandudno excursion, which was blessed with fine weather. It was the paddler's first ever visit to the area, and on account of the conditions encountered later that week, it was to be quite some time before any further plans were drawn up for a return. Here she overtakes Effluent Services Ltd's fully laden chemical waste disposal tanker Scammonden en route from Birkenhead to the 'dump', whilst inward bound is the Icelandic freighter Kljafoss which maintained a regular general cargo service from Iceland to the Weston Point Docks of the British Waterways Board.

Waverley :   *1947 693 grt. Waverley Steam Navigation Co. Ltd. built by A.J. Inglis Ltd. Glasgow*

Scammonden :   *1949 582 grt. Effluent Services Ltd. built by Werf "De Noord" Alblasserdam*

Kljafoss :   *1957 500 grt. Eimskipafelag Reykjavikur H/F. built by Solvesborgs Varv. Solvesborg.*

N.P.B.

WALLASEY 1929 606 grt. The Mayor, Aldermen & Burgesses of the County Borough of Wallasey *20.7.59*

The Wallasey was destined to be the last of the steam ferries on the river, but in the summer of 1959 it was still possible to savour the rich blend of maritime aromas associated with these steamers on the New Brighton, Seacombe or Woodside crossings. With her sistership, Marlowe, delivered only a few weeks later, they revived the policy of naming the passenger vessels after places in the Borough. They were, when built, the largest ferries on the Mersey with passenger certificates for just over 2,230 persons and their hulls were the first in the fleet to incorporate cruiser sterns and the new Flettner balanced type rudders. Originally coal-fired, conversion to oil burning came shortly after the war, with the

practice being to fuel the fleet at Seacombe, taking bunkers from one of the ferries that had earlier charged her tanks at Dingle Oil Jetty. The Wallasey's last passenger sailings were made over the Whitsun holiday in 1963 and, although kept in reserve and steamed for the late summer holiday, she was not actually put back into service again. After laying by for some weeks in the docks, she departed under tow in February 1964 bound for the breakers yard at Ghent. On this July morning she is seen approaching the Liverpool landing stage on the flood tide. In the distance Blue Funnel's Victory type freighter Glaucus (ex Memnon) prepares to dock at Birkenhead.   H.B. Christiansen

53

ROYAL DAFFODIL 1958   6099grt   The Mayor, Aldermen & Burgesses of the County Borough of Wallasey   *February 1970*

The Royal Daffodil II *was the last ferry to be built for the Corporation of Wallasey and was delivered to them by James Lamont & Co. Ltd., of Port Glasgow. The 'II' suffix had been ceremoniously removed in 1968 following the scrapping of a Thames excursion vessel that had until then held the name. This was a time when she was often in the news, as in September 1966 she ran aground north of the Seacombe stage in heavy fog and, just over a year later, had to be beached after a collision with a towed barge, again in foggy conditions. Not long after this photograph of her arriving at the Liverpool Stage was taken, the traditional funnel colours disappeared when the Merseyside Passenger Transport Authority, which had controlled the ferries for the previous two years, replaced these with*

an unhappy combination of primrose yellow and pale blue. A further change came in 1974 when the garish emerald green applied to their buses was adopted.

In 1977 the Royal Daffodil *was withdrawn and sold to a Greek company managed by the Grecomar Shipping Agency (for further details of this organisation's activities see p.21). After a major reconstruction, which increased her length by 15ft. (almost 5 metres) she emerged the following year as the car-ferry* Ioulis Keas II *and employed on services within the Cyclades group of islands. A stern loading ramp was installed two years later and, under new ownership, she has recently been renamed* Agia Kyriaki.   N.P.B.

VIGILANT 1953 728 grt. Mersey Docks & Harbour Board.

The Vigilant *was a familiar feature of the Pier Head scene from her completion by John I. Thornycroft & Co. Ltd., at Southampton in 1953 to her demise 25 years later. Besides salvage work and a fire fighting role using the monitors installed on her mastheads and wheelhouse roof – she was also utilised for survey and buoy maintenance. Operating on a rotational basis with her near sister* Salvor, *one of these craft was always maintained in a continuous state of readiness. Being oil fired steamers, propelled by a pair of triple expansion engines, the cost of such a modus operandum escalated as the 70's progressed.*

Therefore it came as no surprise, when a single diesel powered replacement vessel was launched from a Dutch shipyard in May 1978. In order that the newcomer could become the fourth holder of the name: Vigilant, *the steamer was renamed* Staunch *in the same year, although she was never to operate under this identity. On November 30th 1978, together with the* Salvor, *she was towed to Garston Beach for demolition by Pemberton & Carlyon (Shipbreakers) Ltd.*

N.P.B.

MAMMOTH 1920 1,524 grt.
Mersey Docks and Harbour Co.

10.4.73

Whether placing heavy lift export cargoes on board ships, or attending on heavy maintenance and repair work around the dock estate, the floating crane **Mammoth** *was a familiar sight on either side of the river. Built in 1920, she seemed over sixty years later, to be an inseparable part of the dockland scene. A number of interesting, but apocryphal, stories have surrounded her early history. The facts are that she was originally ordered by the Tsarist government of Russia but, following the 1917 revolution, she was not delivered and was eventually purchased from the builders at Schiedam, near Rotterdam, by the Mersey Docks & Harbour Board in 1920. With her 200' (60 metre) high jib and 200 tonne lifting capacity, the* **Mammoth** *was one of the largest cranes afloat for many years. Triple expansion steam engines powered the crane section and also served as propulsion units. With a nominal speed of 4 knots, she only moved under her own power within the docks and her river passages were made with a small flotilla of tugs. The* **Mammoth's** *career on the Mersey finally ended in 1987 when a new 250 tonne capacity crane, the* **Mersey Mammoth,** *also built in Holland, replaced her. She left the Mersey bound for Oxelosund where her new Swedish owners were reported to be intending to replace her steam machinery with diesels. However, she is still recorded as retaining her original engines and it would be interesting to learn of her present disposition. Here the* **Mammoth** *is completing a lift onto the foredeck of the* **Ebani,** *one of a succession of Elder Dempster ships to serve in Blue Funnel colours on their Far East service for a short time in 1972.*

P.H.B.

EDMUND GARDNER No. 2 Pilot Cutter.   1953   734 grt.   Mersey Docks & Harbour Company.

25.9.80

One of three similar diesel electric pilot tenders all built by Phillip & Son Ltd. at Dartmouth between 1951 and 1958 for the Mersey Docks & Harbour Board. Although the Liverpool pilots were self employed, the 'Board maintained the Pilotage service, stationing cutters at Point Lynas, Anglesey and at the Mersey Bar. Each boat would spend a week on station, with the third being spare; hand over being carried out every Thursday at Liverpool Landing Stage. Gradually, fast launches replaced the tenders, first at Point Lynas in November 1974, and eventually the Bar station succumbed in 1982.

*Fortuitously, No. 2 was acquired by the Merseyside Maritime Museum for preservation, where she is now to be found on public display on the blocks in the Canning No. 1 Drydock at Liverpool. Although splendidly restored with all machinery still operational, it is thought very unlikely that she will ever put to sea again, due to the considerable expense that would be incurred. In this photo, No. 2 has just left the Landing Stage to relieve on the Bar Station. Note the **Mona's Isle** and **Manxman** in the winter layup in Birkenhead's Morpeth Dock.*

N.P.B.

57

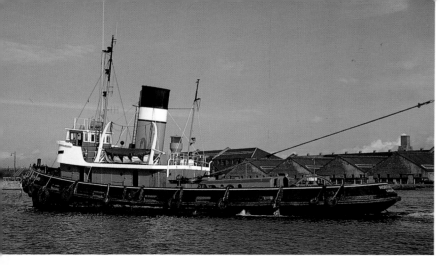

ALEXANDRA TOWING CO. LTD.

These four photographs of Alexandra towing vessels illustrate the evolution of the tug over the last three decades.

The North End (1957/215 grt) – **Upper Left** *– was typical of the many steam tugs built during the course of the 1950's which, whilst incorporating various refinements were, in principle, little advanced on the pre-war designs. She was one of seven "North" tugs delivered between 1956 and 1959 and these were the last steamers built for towage on the Mersey and indeed in Britain. Their steam reciprocation engines gave an equivalent of 870 B.H.P. The Trafalgar (1966/173 grt) –* **Upper Right** *– was the last of the traditional design of tugs for the company which, although diesel powered, were clearly descended from their steam powered predecessors. One of a group of eight generally similar vessels, the*

Trafalgar had an updated engine giving an output of 1,350 B.H.P. The Brocklebank, one of the earlier examples of this series, built by Yarwood's at Northwich, is actively preserved at the Maritime Museum. The next new tugs to be ordered for the Mersey fleet were a group of four significantly larger vessels, which have often been employed around the coast of Britain and beyond. These have a single engine developing 2,190 B.H.P. and giving a bollard pull of 39 tonnes. The Crosby (1972/272 grt) – **Lower Left** *– was the second of the series to enter service and is currently based on the Mersey. The Bramley Moore (1984/336 grt) –* **Lower Right** *– was built by McTay's at Bromborough and is typical of the modern sophisticated tugs now in service. Twin diesel engines producing a total 3,444 B.H.P. each drive a directional impeller unit of the Voith-Schneider type and give a manoeuvrability undreamt of in the days of the steamers.*

All P.H.B.

NORTH QUAY 1956 219 grt. Alexandra Towing Co. Ltd.

December '69

One of a series of seven fine looking oil fired steam tugs delivered to the company between 1956 and 1959, North Quay built by Scott & Sons, of Bowling in October 1956, was the fourth to enter service. With their 'North' names, they introduced a new system of nomenclature to the fleet which had hitherto adopted names of Merseyside Docks or local areas where the vessels were employed. The company disposed of all of their steamers on the Mersey in 1972 the North Quay going to Italian buyers as the Terralba for use in Sardinia, where she is believed to be still in service. Other vessels visible in this Langton Dock scene are the Mersey Docks & Harbour Board's survey launch Mersey Inspector alongside the ornate Langton Graving Dock pumphouse and the dredger Mersey Compass at the East end of Brocklebank Branch Dock.

N.P.B.

59

HEATH COCK 1958 193 grt. Liverpool Screw Towing Co. Ltd.

23.8.70

The first motor tug to be built for the 'Cock Tugs' fleet, and also the first tug of that means of propulsion to be specifically built for Mersey service. As with many of her fleet mates, she was built locally by Cammell Laird & Co. Ltd., together with a slightly younger sister – West Cock. Although many of the traditional features favoured by her owners were still incorporated, for example the gaff and weather cock vane on the mast, with a nicely proportioned riveted funnel, there were also innovations such as the wrap around totally enclosed wheelhouse and the absence of a conventional life boat – inflatable rafts being supplied in place thereof. In December 1966, the fleet passed into the ownership of Alexandra Towing Co. Ltd., and this must be one of the last photographs of the Heath Cock in her original guise as repainting and renaming followed very soon after, in the

autumn of that year. As the Collingwood, and for the last few months Collingwood II, she served in Alexandra colours until 1981 when all five of the remaining former Cock tugs were sold to the Piraeus based Vernicos Shipping Co. Ltd., and given 'Vernicos' prefixed names. However, her migration to warmer climes was not to be for whilst in tow deadship of the former Canada (ex. Pea Cock), together with the former Formby (ex. Weather Cock), all three were lost near Solva on the South Wales coast when the lead tug fouled her propeller in bad weather.

Other shipping visible in this view are the Ben-my-Chree and Lady of Mann at the Landing Stage with the sand dredger Norwest rounding-up mid river prior to locking in at the Waterloo entrance.

P.H.B.

J. H. LAMEY 1964 216grt. J. H. Lamey Ltd. with the SPYROS L. 1940 2,209grt. S. Lalis & Co. Ltd. *June 70*

The J. H. Lamey is seen here escorting the Greek flagged steamer Spyros L., as they approach the Duke Street lifting bridge on the way through from the East to the West Float. She was the second of five motor tugs built for the Lamey fleet to have the distinctive twin exhaust uptakes in place of a conventional funnel. Whilst greatly improving visibility aft, the uptakes were too narrow to carry the company's colours and consequently in the late 'sixties the Lamey houseflag was applied to the bridge wings. The fleet was taken over by Alexandra Towing in 1968 and two years later the J. H. Lamey was renamed Hornby, as which she served until 1984 when she passed to owners based in Northern Ireland who renamed her Samuel F.

Still visible on the bow of the Spyros L. is her former name Angelo, as which she was built

for Ellerman's Wilson Line by Swan, Hunter & Wigham Richardson at Newcastle. Powered by a triple expansion steam engine with a low pressure exhaust turbine, she was originally coal fired and converted to oil burning in 1955. Sold in 1963 she was initially renamed Nevada II becoming the Spyros L. later the same year. Laid up in Piraeus in February 1971, she was transferred to the Cypriot registry and renamed Manos I, but never traded as such and was broken up there in March, 1973.

In the background are the two Dutch vessels; the coaster Ali Damhof on Buchanan's Jetty and, in the distance, the bulk carrier Asterope at the Liverpool Grain Storage and Transit Company's berth.

A. Spedding **61**

H.B. CHRISTIANSEN 20.7.59

REA TOWING CO. LTD.

The Carlgarth *(1922/ 179 grt.)* **(above)** and Yorkgarth *(1923/179 grt)* **(right)** were two of the first six tugs built for the new company formed by Rea's in 1922. With the exception of a wartime loss, all were to have a long association with the river. The Carlgarth was the first to be sold, passing to new owners at Cardiff in 1961 and the following year the Yorkgarth was scrapped at Preston. The Applegarth *(1951/231 grt)* **(below left)**, one of the last steamers in the fleet, had the misfortune to sink twice in her career, on the second occasion in 1960 with the loss of all her crew. She was returned to service, however, and in 1971 was sold to Holyhead Towing Co. Ltd. Renamed Afon Cefni she passed to Greek buyers two years later, becoming the Achilles. The Foylegarth *(1958/208 grt)* **(below right)**, was acquired in 1969, together with two sisters, from Johnston Warren Lines Ltd., part of the Furness, Withy group who, up to that time, had maintained a small tug fleet on the Mersey to handle their own vessels. In 1983 she was bought by the Falmouth Towage Ltd. and, as their St. Budoc, is still in service.

▼ J.M. WILLIAMS 11.4.70   ▼ N.P.B.   ▲ J.CLARKSON

WILLOWGARTH 1959 230 grt and BEECHGARTH 1964 213 grt. Rea Towing Co. Ltd.

Seen at low water off Langton entrance, these two tugs represented the second and fifth respectively in their owners motor tug replacement programme. There were three distinct designs amongst the five vessels, the first four being built by the Appledore yard of P.K. Harris & Co. Ltd., whilst **Beechgarth** *was built locally on the River Weaver by W.J. Yarwood & Sons Ltd. She was the only one of the five to be equipped with two masts and*

as such was easily distinguishable. At the time of writing, **Beechgarth** *is still an operational member of the fleet, although she now bears the new Cory funnel markings. The* **Willowgarth***, however, was sold to Greeks in 1986, becoming the* **Thiseus** *for service at Thessalonika. The rubble in the background, is the remains of the old Canada entrance, which the then 'state of the art' Langton Lock replaced in 1963.*

29.6.75

P.H.B.

63

PEGU   1961   5,764 grt.   Guinea Gulf Line Ltd.

Farewell to the Mersey! – outward bound from Langton Lock.   The Pegu had a particularly colourful career within the Ocean Group carrying in turn the funnel markings of Henderson, Elder Dempster, Blue Funnel and finally Guinea Gulf Lines, under which she was one of the last vessels to be placed in the ownership of this famous Liverpool concern. As can be seen, she retained the Glasgow registry from former days with Paddy Henderson's British & Burmese Steam Navigation Co. Ltd., and like most of her consorts, this open shelter deck motor freighter was a product of Lithgows Ltd. Port Glasgow yard. Her days under the British flag ended on the West African service, and she was sold in 1980, her name simply being altered at a single stroke to Regu.   Later that same year, she

transferred to the Cypriot flag to become the Joelle. With one further change of name still under the flag of Cyprus to Nicol Mylo in 1982, she met her end in the hands of Taiwanese shipbreakers, arriving at Kaohsiung on 7/11/83.

The remains of Henderson's previous Pegu are still visible at low water on the revetment in Liverpool's Crosby Channel, which she ran on to during the night of November 24th 1939 whilst on a voyage from Glasgow to Rangoon via Liverpool to join an outward bound convoy. On entering the channel she had been forced to take evasive action to avoid two other ships that had been in collision.

N.P.B.